HI

TENNIS

JOHN CRACE   Illustrated by HELEN AVERLEY

First published in 1997 by
Appletree Press Ltd.
19-21 Alfred Street, Belfast BT2 8DL.
Tel. +44 (0)1232 243074 Fax. +44 (0)1232 256756

A Little History of Tennis

A catalogue record for this book is available
from the British Library.

ISBN 0-86281-628-9

9 8 7 6 5 4 3 2 1

Contents

Introduction

With the spread of the Industrial Revolution and the resulting growth of, and interest in, leisure pursuits among the increasingly affluent middle classes, England was ready for tennis in 1874. What no-one could have foreseen was just how quickly the game would take off. Within three years the first open championships were held at Wimbledon, and before the end of the century the game had spread worldwide. Nowadays, thanks to its appeal to both sexes and to the enormous TV coverage the sport receives, tennis can justifiably claim to be one of the most popular games in the world.

Jeu de paume

The Origins of the Game

Among the many inventions of the Victorian era were the lawn mower, the garden roller and the rubber ball, and it was these, as much as the inspiration of Walter Wingfield, a retired army officer, who introduced the game of Sphairistike to the gardens of England's leisured classes, that marked the birth of the modern game of lawn tennis in 1874. But the ancient game of tennis or *jeu de paume*, as it was known, and to which lawn tennis is closely related, dates back to the twelfth century, and its history is interwoven with the social fabric of medieval Europe.

It is not certain whether *jeu de paume* originated in France or Italy, but, as its name suggests, it was in France that the game achieved its greatest popularity. In the early days the game was played by hitting the ball with the palm of the hand; some time later a glove was developed to protect the hand, but it was not until the fifteenth century that the first primitive rackets came into use.

Almost from the very beginning, *jeu de paume* existed in two forms, *longue paume* and *courte paume*, the former being played on a specially prepared open space, the latter in an area enclosed by walls. Neither was played with any net or line markings, but unsurprisingly, given the space requirements, it was *courte paume* that took off in the towns and cities. The earliest enthusiasts appear to have been ecclesiastical students playing against the cloister walls, but, because most people could not afford to hire a court, within a comparatively short period of time *courte paume* had become firmly identified as the game of royalty and the aristocracy. The first monarch known to have played *courte paume* was Louis X (1314-16) of France, who died after catching a chill while cooling off after a particularly energetic game.

Jeu de paume crossed the English Channel to Great Britain sometime in the mid-fourteenth century, where it quickly became known as tennis. There has been much speculation as to how the game came to be so called: the most likely explanation is that players used to call out *'tenez'* (hold) before serving. Tennis soon gained the same popularity in Britain as it had in France, so that by 1365 it was felt necessary to pass laws prohibiting such 'vain games' in order to promote more war-like pursuits, such as archery. Not that these laws applied to the king himself. If we are to believe William Shakespeare, then Henry V (1413-22) was more than well acquainted with the game, for when the French Dauphin sent him some tennis balls as a present, Henry replies:

Henry V

When we have matched our rackets to these balls,
We will, in France, by God's grace, play a set.
Henry V, Act I, Scene II.

The sixteenth century was tennis's golden age. Henry VII (1485-1509) was a frequent player, as was his son Henry VIII (1509-47), and during their reigns a large number of courts were built, including those in the royal palaces of Westminster, Windsor, Whitehall, Hampton Court and St James's.

The game enjoyed enormous success throughout Europe, especially in Italy, Spain, the Netherlands, the German states and the Austro-Hungarian empire, but it was in France that its greatest expansion took place. By the end of the reign of Louis XII (1498-1515) there were over 40 courts in his home town

of Orleans, and his successor, François I (1515-47), continued the good work. Wherever he travelled he built courts, including those at the Louvre and Fontainebleau, and he even insisted on having a tennis court built on board his four-masted warship, *La Grande Françoise*. In 1571 King Charles IX (1560-74) formalised the constitution of the Corporation of Tennis Professionals, and by the end of the century there were over 250 courts in Paris, with some 7,000 people directly employed in the tennis industry.

This heyday of *jeu de paume*, or *real tennis*, also saw the publication in 1555 of the first known book on tennis, *Trattato del Guico della Palla*, written by an Italian priest, Antonio Scaino da Salo, and in 1592 a French tennis professional named Forbet wrote the first known rules of the game. But by the middle of the next century, the game's popularity in France was on the wane. In 1657 the Dutch ambassador reported that the number of courts in Paris had fallen to 114, and by 1783 these had declined to just 13. The French Revolution of 1789 brought a complete, if temporary, halt to the game, but not before the tennis court at Versailles became immortalised in French history as the place where the Third Estate, who had been banned by the king from their usual meeting-place, vowed not to disband until France had a proper constitution. However, even after the revolution was over, a combination of the Napoleonic wars and public apathy ensured that tennis never regained its former status.

It was a similar story back in England. King Charles I (1625-49) was an avid tennis player and didn't even let a small matter like the Civil War detract from his pleasures. Indeed, in 1643 he got special permission from Parliament for material for a tennis suit to be sent from London to Oxford, where he was in the habit of playing regularly with Prince Rupert. Tennis playing was suspended in the country after Oliver Cromwell's victory and the execution of Charles I, but the Restoration of the monarchy under Charles II, the eldest son of Charles I, saw a brief revival of the game.

However, the physique of the Hanoverian kings did not readily lend itself to physical pastimes, and their lack of interest and patronage heralded a steady decline in the popularity of tennis - a decline that may have been exacerbated by the death of the Prince of Wales in 1751 after he was hit by a tennis ball. Thus, although 'rackets' and 'fives' - two offshoots of tennis - had their devotees, tennis was all but dead throughout Europe by the early years of the nineteenth century.

By the middle of the century Britain's industrial dominance within Europe had given rise to a new prosperity, and from this emerged a new middle class with leisure time on their hands. During this period, many new *real tennis* courts were built throughout the country as the game underwent a renaissance, and in the summer of 1859 a Birmingham solicitor named Harry Gem and his great friend, Augurio Perera, both keen 'rackets' players, decided to experiment with an outdoor version of tennis. This was played using a rubber ball on the croquet lawn of Perera's home in the Birmingham suburb of Edgbaston, and from these tentative beginnings the modern game of lawn tennis was born.

Harry Gem was nothing if not an enthusiast, and his version of the game became so popular amongst his circle of friends and acquaintances over the next 12 years that he and Perera formed the Leamington Lawn Tennis Club in 1872, the first club, so far as is known, to be devoted exclusively to lawn tennis. Yet Gem is not remembered as the father of the modern game; that honour goes to Major Walter Wingfield, whose bust today stands proudly in the entrance to the Lawn Tennis Association in London.

The first record of Major Wingfield playing his version of tennis dates back to 1869, but it was for his introduction and patenting of his game *Sphairistike* in 1874 that he achieved his pre-eminence. Wingfield was a natural entrepreneur and *Sphairistike* from the Greek word meaning 'ball game'

Henry VIII was a keen courte paume *player, and built several courts.*

quickly caught the imagination of Victorian England. The sets, comprising rubber balls, four rackets and netting, sold for 5 guineas, and by the following year Wingfield was happy to boast a distinguished list of people who had bought one, a list that included 11 princes and princesses, 7 dukes, 17 marquis and marchionesses, 54 earls, 6 countesses, 105 viscounts, 41 barons, 44 ladies, 44 honourables, 5 right honourables and 55 baronets and knights.

Not surprisingly, many others tried to cash in on the outdoor game's new-found popularity by producing their own version, and this proliferation meant that there were soon almost as many different games of tennis, each with its own set of rules, as there were players. Clearly some regulation was needed and, in the absence of any other legitimate authority, it fell to the Marylebone Cricket Club (MCC), which was also the governing body for rackets and real tennis, to adjudicate on the rules for lawn tennis in March 1875. Many of the attributes of Sphairistike, notably the hour-glass court, were retained and the new rules were broadly accepted. However, the MCC had only put forward these new rules as broad guide-lines, saying that the size of the court could vary according to players' capabilities and the quality of the grass; it was left to the rules committee of the first ever Wimbledon championship to standardise the rules into a form which has remained fundamentally the same to this day.

The All England Croquet Club had been founded in Worple Road, Wimbledon, in 1869, but within six years it was on its last legs. Thus in 1875 when one of the founders, a Mr. Henry Jones, suggested that the club should incorporate lawn tennis, the idea was accepted with alacrity. Two years later the game had thrived to such an extent that there were no croquet players left on the club's committee. In the same year, 1877, Jones suggested that the club should play host to a lawn tennis tournament that was open to all-comers, with a silver challenge cup worth 25 guineas to be awarded to the winner. With such a valuable prize at stake, it was vital to formulate a standard set of rules, and so the modern game of lawn tennis finally emerged. What is more, the first Wimbledon championship transformed the game almost overnight from a gentle recreational pastime into an international sport.

The Worldwide Growth
of Tennis

The growing appetite among the middle classes for holidaying in continental Europe, together with the large number of British colonies and outposts across the globe and the attraction of a game that men and women could play together, made the worldwide spread of lawn tennis almost inevitable once the game had caught on at home. What must have come as a surprise to all concerned was just how quickly that spread took place.

Tennis came to the USA via Bermuda, where legend has it that a man called Thomas Middleton imported a tennis set from England in 1873. Middleton reputedly decided that the game was far too energetic for his liking and handed over his equipment to a neighbour, Sir Brownlow Gray, who marked out a court at his home in Clermont. The words 'legend' and 'reputedly' are used advisedly, because there is only hearsay evidence to confirm this story. What is certain is that Sir Brownlow Gray's daughter, Mary, took to the game with a passion, and was the winner of an open tennis championship, albeit one with only three entrants, that took place at Admiralty House in April 1876.

It was another Mary who was responsible for bringing the game to the USA. Mary Ewing Outerbridge was visiting Bermuda in January 1874 and became fascinated by the game. She returned to New York with a set of equipment in February and, with the help of her brother, A. Emilius Outerbridge, established a tennis court at the Staten Island Cricket and Baseball Club. Later on that year, a court was built at the home of William Appleton, who lived in the Boston suburb of Nahant, and tennis gradually spread across New England over the next two years. There were some, apparently, who watched this British game under the misapprehension that they were watching cricket, and, as in England, various versions of tennis were being played. But in September 1880 the first open tennis meeting, grandly entitled the Championship of America, was held at the Staten Island Club and was won by a visiting Englishman named O.E. Woodhouse. The following year the United States Lawn Tennis Association was formed in Newport, Rhode Island, and one of its first actions was to standardise the rules by accepting those of the All England Club at Wimbledon.

However, while recreational and championship tennis were taking off simultaneously in Britain and the USA, it was as a social game that tennis initially found favour on mainland Europe. The French were happy enough playing the odd back-

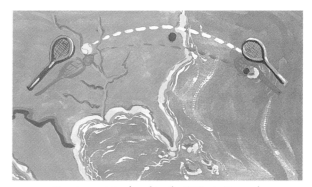

Tennis was introduced to the USA via Bermuda

garden game of *Sphairistike*, but it was the visiting British who were largely responsible for establishing the original mainstream tennis clubs. A group of English holiday-makers established the Dinard Lawn Tennis Club, and the warm winter weather of the Côte d'Azur attracted a large number of migrant enthusiasts who leapt at the chance of playing all the year round on the sand courts of the Beau Site Club in Cannes, and on those at Nice, Monte Carlo and Menton. In the early days it was only in Paris that the game achieved any importance, and two courts were built at the Racing Club de France in 1882. Only towards the end of the decade did other tennis clubs begin to proliferate.

The Italian Riviera proved just as popular as the French with those wishing to play throughout the year, but the spread

The Côte d'Azur offered enthusiasts year round tennis

of the game to Sweden owed nothing to climatic conditions. That honour went to King Gustav V who, as Crown Prince, imported a tennis set from England in 1879, and his royal patronage increased the game's popularity. Gustav ordered a court to be built at Saro, an island resort where he used to holiday each summer, and within a couple of years there were courts for all-year-round play in Stockholm.

Where grass was not suitable as a surface, courts were made out of gravel, asphalt concrete, sand and brick dust, and the game quickly colonised the rest of Europe. Championships began in France in 1889, in Belgium in 1895, in Switzerland in 1898, and in Portugal in 1900. A championship of Europe was played at a different venue each year from 1899 until after World War I, and tennis was included as one of the sports for the inaugural modern Olympic Games held at Athens in 1896.

Tennis spread just as quickly in the southern hemisphere, and the game rapidly developed into an organised sport. In Australia, Victoria held a state championship in 1880, New South Wales followed suit in 1885, and in the same year these two states began a biannual series of inter-state matches that has survived to the present day. Queensland and South Australia both established their state championships in 1890, with Tasmania following in 1893 and Western Australia two years later, but it wasn't until 1905, when all the states became incorporated into the Australian nation, that the first national championships were held.

Across the Tasman Sea in New Zealand, the game arrived

sometime in the 1880s. One of the first clubs to be formed was the Parnell LTC of Auckland which, like the All England Club before it, had begun life as a croquet club. The first national championships were held in 1886 and have been played every year since.

Tennis was a more low-key affair in South Africa. It began in the late 1870s in Natal where, as in so many other places, it was a pastime for expatriate Englishmen, and the first tournament was held in Durban in 1871. Thereafter the game developed slowly throughout the country over the next decade, but that does not mean it was played to a poor standard. Teddy Williams, a young South African, won many tournaments and in 1884 reached the final of the Wimbledon men's doubles. By 1891 the game was sufficiently established for the first South African championships to be staged.

Thus, in the space of little more than 25 years, tennis had grown from a figment of Major Wingfield's imagination to a worldwide game, and by the beginning of the twentieth century it had truly won the right to be described as one of the most popular of all international sports.

The Development of the Game

The first international tennis match took place at Wimbledon in July 1883 between C.M. and J.S. Clark of the USA and the Renshaw twins, William and Ernest, representing Great Britain. For the record, the Renshaws came out on top, but by far the most important feature of the match was the precedent it set. The very next year Americans played in the Wimbledon championships for the first time; five years later E.G. Meers became the first British person to play in the American championships, and within a short period of time it had become relatively common for the best players to travel to overseas tournaments. One of the knock-on effects of this was that tennis quickly became a focal point for national pride and rivalries, such that in 1900 the Davis Cup competition was established.

The Davis Cup began life as a men's match exclusively between Great Britain and the USA; within a few years France, Belgium and Germany were also competing, and by the outbreak of World War II the number of countries taking part had risen to 41. By 1967 this figure had reached 62. Yet the development of the game is not just the history of the men's game. One of the major factors in the speed at which tennis developed, was the influence of women. In the later decades of the nineteenth century there had, in western Europe and the USA, been a growing political acceptance of the rights of women, and, having spent centuries being denied the pleasures of "unladylike" competition, women saw tennis as a game at which they too could excel.

Indeed, women's tennis has, in many ways, mirrored the emancipation of their sex. In the very early days of the game, the competitions open to women were few and far between, and were accorded far less status than their male counterparts. The first women's tournament took place in Ireland in 1879, with Wimbledon following suit five years later. In 1888 the USLTA refused to sanction women's tennis, but was forced to rescind this decision only a year later, no doubt recognising an unstoppable force when they saw it. The Philadelphia Cricket Club had already held the first women's tournament in 1887. American women were made to pay for their presumption by playing five-set matches, and it wasn't until 1902 that this anomaly was rectified and women's tennis was limited to three sets as had been played at Wimbledon from the start.

With the suffragette movement growing in strength and women playing a major role in the work-force during World War I, women's tennis grew in popularity. This was perhaps best symbolised by Suzanne Lenglen, the winner of seven Wimbledon titles on the trot in the 1920s, whose looks and

Suzanne Lenglen

talent made her a sporting icon for both the men and the women of her generation. Lenglen almost single-handedly turned tennis from a connoisseur's game into a mass spectator sport, and her impact on women's tennis was almost immediate. In 1923 the Wightman Cup, the women's equivalent of the Davis Cup, was inaugurated, though this competition remained a contest between the USA and Great Britain. For a truly international event, women's tennis had to wait until after World War II for the creation of the Federation Cup.

The game's administrators were hard pushed to keep up with the rapid development of the sport in the early years, and this has remained the case to the present day. Far from governing and controlling the sport, as was originally intended, the governing bodies of tennis have a long history of failing to predict changing moods and fashions and, more often than not, of being forced to respond to them. It is hard to blame the early administrators too much; they were, by and large, enthusiastic amateurs who could have had no idea of how the game would spread. One cannot be so sanguine about those who came later, when the game was already international, but perhaps sometimes it is difficult to change something that started in such a haphazard way.

In 1888, seven years after the USLTA was established, the British Lawn Tennis Association (LTA) was formed to oversee the running of the British game. Curiously, the LTA also took

charge of the game in many other countries, such that by the early 1900s it represented 24 nations and was effectively running the game worldwide, with the exception of the USA which continued to follow the auspices of the USLTA. Clearly something needed to change: the British LTA could not look after vested interests at home and abroad, and another body was needed to oversee tennis worldwide.

In 1911 Douane Williams, an American acting as secretary to the Swiss national association, proposed the creation of the International Lawn Tennis Federation. This was adopted after a meeting in Paris the following year and the ILTF was born. Surprisingly, the USA did not number among the 12 founder members. Despite recognising that the tennis authorities needed to adapt to the game's international stature, the USLTA preferred to retain its parochial stance, and it wasn't until 1923 that it opted to join. Even then the ILTF was forced to pay for the USA's entry. One of the ILTF's first acts in 1913 had been to institute three world championships the Hard Court, the Covered Court and the Grass all of which took place in Europe. The USA took this as an insult to the quality of its own championships, and insisted on the abandonment of the world championships. Luckily, the game was bigger than the administrators and no long-term damage was done.

In truth, there was probably little that could have stopped the growth of the game. Despite the devastation and destruction of World War I (1914-18), it was virtually business as usual by 1919, and by the following year there were almost 50 per cent more competitions than there had been in 1913. This proliferation in the number of tournaments reflected the game's popularity. The All England Club was forced to relocate from Worple Road to a bigger ground at Church Road in Wimbledon to accommodate public demand, and the same thing happened in the USA and in France: a new 17,000-seater stadium was built at Forest Hills, Long Island, in 1923, and five years later the vast concrete arena of the Stade Roland Garros was opened just outside Paris.

Given the spectator interest and the individual nature of the sport, it was inevitable that the first proper generation of tennis superstars should appear at this time. Their names reflected the emergence of the French and the Germans in the 1920s as rivals to the American, British and Australian dominance of the world game. Indeed, while only one American, William Tilden, has become immortalised as an all-time great, no less than five French tennis players of the same period are remembered with equal respect and affection. They are the inimitable Suzanne Lenglen and the Davis Cup quartet of René Lacoste, Jean Barotra, Henri Cochet and Jacques Brugnon - otherwise known as the four musketeers.

Where idolatry leads, so money follows, and the administration of the period from World War I up to the early 1970s is characterised by both weakness and hypocrisy in its attitudes to players' earnings. Prior to World War I, tennis had retained its amateur status, to the extent that in 1909 some British players had been censured for accepting hospitality from the King of Portugal. However, all this changed after the war. Many of the big tournaments that were administered by the ILTF, such as Wimbledon, the US Championships, the French Open and the Australian Open, were only open to amateur players, but there is little doubt that some of the best

Bill Tilden

players competing in these events, Tilden and Lenglen included, received substantial financial rewards from the game which the authorities deliberately chose to ignore. However, officially at least, the division between amateur and professional status remained deep, though by the end of the 1930s there was a growing preference for turning professional - ironically precipitated by Lenglen and Tilden's very public defection to the professional ranks in the late 1920s.

Throughout the 1930s this defection continued, and Henri Cochet, Ellsworth Vines, Fred Perry, Don Budge and Bobby Riggs all changed their status after winning Wimbledon. The same pattern continued after World War II, with players like Jack Kramer, Pancho Gonzales, Frank Sedgman and Ken

Rosewall all opting to join the ranks of professionals playing big-money games at Madison Square Garden in New York. Still the ILTF remained committed to amateur tennis - a stance that became increasingly absurd.

Even before World War II, it was apparent that playing tennis at the highest level was a full-time occupation. It demanded great stamina and fitness, endless practice and the time to play in various tournaments around the world, all of which was anathema to amateurism. After the war, as the demands of top-level tennis intensified, the situation became even more farcical. During this period, which saw the dominance of the Americans and latterly the Australians, players who were clearly full-time athletes, and well paid for it, were presented to the public at the major championships as true amateurs even though they had no visible means of support. The ILTF tried to reconcile the situation by allowing amateur tennis players 'expenses' for a certain number of days per year, but this fudging of the issue only highlighted the absurdity of the situation.

As more players, such as the great Rod Laver, changed status, and professional tournaments gained popularity, many people in the early 1960s, most notably the British, US and Australian LTAs, who wanted the best players to appear at their tournaments, sought to make all tournaments open to professionals and amateurs alike. Predictably, the ILTF resisted for as long as possible, but in 1968 open tennis was born. This wasn't quite the end of the matter, though. In 1971 a group of tennis promoters, known as World Championship Tennis (WCT), tried to force the ILTF to give professional players a larger slice of the money, and threatened to set up a rival tour. The ILTF rejected most of the WCT's claims, but a year later the two organisations agreed a compromise that has allowed tennis to thrive ever since.

Women's tennis has always had its stars - Lenglen, Helen Wills Moody and Maureen 'Mo' Connolly immediately come to mind - but it was slower to reach the technical and physical heights of the men's game. It wasn't until the 1960s that women's tennis matured, through the likes of Margaret Court and Billie Jean King, and their mantle has been carried forward from the 1970s to the present day by Chris Evert, Martina Navratilova and Steffi Graf.

In the same period men's tennis has thrown up some remarkable champions, such as Ilie Nastase, Jimmy Connors, Bjorn Borg, John McEnroe, Boris Becker and Pete Sampras, but perhaps the most notable feature of the modern era has

been the financial explosion of the game. Apart from the prize money on offer, both at the major events and at countless minor satellite tournaments, sponsorship and endorsements have turned tennis players into some of the highest paid sportsmen and women in the world. Even a player outside the top 100 in the world rankings can expect to earn over $100,000 per year, and for those near the top the sky is the limit. In October 1996 Gabriella Sabatini retired from the game at the comparatively young age of 26. Thought by many never to have fulfilled her potential, she won only one major championship. Even so, in the course of her career she earned over $6 million in prize money and an estimated $13 million in endorsements. Goodness knows what Walter Wingfield would have made of that!

The Equipment

Every player since the Middle Ages has searched for that elusive racket that will give him or her the edge over opponents, and the history of the tennis racket is the story of whim, imagination and technological innovation.

The earliest games of *jeu de paume* were played either bare-handed or with the aid of a white leather glove, but by the fifteenth century the first primitive tennis racket was in use. This was a hollowed out wooden bat covered with parchment, known as a *battoir*. A century later the first recognisable rackets appeared; these were initially strung diagonally, but were soon replaced by ones with the horizontal and vertical string design with which we are familiar today.

The first rackets used for lawn tennis in the 1880s were crafted out of wood and, unsurprisingly, resembled those used for real tennis. However, the rather flat, blunt end of the racket was unable to cope with the tensions in the stringing, frequently causing the frame to split and break, and soon this design gave way to the present-day oval shape. But the overall size of the original rackets barely changed for nearly 100 years: in the 1920s a British player named F.W. Donnisthorpe built himself a giant racket, which he claimed improved his volleying, but his design never caught on presumably because most players found it to be more of a hindrance than a help.

Early tennis rackets were strung with leather. Other materials, such as piano wire, were experimented with before gut, produced from the stomach and intestinal linings of sheep and cows, was adopted as standard. Initially all rackets were strung by hand, and as a result the evenness and the tension of the stringing was variable, but by the late 1930s the first primitive stringing machines were in commercial use. Their arrival heralded a minor revolution in the game. It had always been known that string tension could affect the power, spin, touch and control with which the ball was hit, but while players had always tried to customise their rackets, they were limited in their range of options, and in any case there was no scientific way of adjusting a racket to the precise feel and set-up required. The stringing machine meant that players could now have their rackets custom made, and within 20 years the ILTF was forced to step in to prevent professionals seeking an unfair competitive advantage, by insisting that all racket strings should be evenly spaced and that they should not tamper with the flight of the ball.

A few professionals dallied with the idea of metal in the

1920s, but the first major material innovation came in the

White leather jeu de paume *gauntlets*

1930s with lamination. Where previously rackets had been made out of a single wood (ash), lamination allowed strips of woods such as ash, beech and hickory, each of differing weight and stiffness, to be bonded together to make stronger, lighter rackets. However, the period since the mid-1960s has witnessed the greatest changes in racket design as new technology has thrown up new materials. Nowadays, rackets are made out of strong, lightweight alloys such as glass fibre, graphite, Boron and Kevlar, all of which allow players an unprecedented range of control. Indeed, one of the spin-offs of using these modern materials was that their lighter weight enabled manufacturers and players to experiment once more with outsize rackets, and for the very first time the ILTF was forced, in July 1981, to lay down regulations to fix the maximum width and length of tennis rackets.

No less important to the development of the modern game

has been the changing design of the tennis ball. In the Middle Ages, tennis balls were generally made of wool or dog's hair wrapped in leather, and their design and specifications were taken extremely seriously. A book published in 1767 by F.A. de Garsault, entitled *Art du Paumier-Raquetier et de la Paume*, goes to great lengths to explain the manufacturing process, and even lists three different types of tennis balls. However, even though a tennis ball might last for years, it didn't bounce very high, and it was the invention of the indiarubber ball that precipitated the introduction of lawn tennis.

The earliest tennis balls were made of red rubber, but by the time the first Wimbledon championships were held, they were covered in white wool, which was stitched over the rubber core using carpet thread. They were inflated by a gas pellet that was placed inside. By about 1924, new adhesives meant that the stitching could be dispensed with; these stitchless balls were faster than before but less responsive to the effects of spin. Tennis balls became faster still in 1931 after the pressure was increased, and again after World War II when the wool covering was replaced by a mixture of wool and man-made fibres. Since then their size, weight and compression have become standardised and the only noticeable changes to ball design have been cosmetic. Where once they were all white, nowadays one is hard pushed to find any white balls. Even Wimbledon, that last bastion of tradition, switched over to yellow balls in 1986.

Wimbledon, Worple Road, in the 1890s

The Grand Slam Events

Hundreds of professional tennis tournaments are played each year around the world, but four stand head and shoulders above the rest. They are Wimbledon, the US Open, the French Open and the Australian Open, known collectively as the Grand Slam events. Players who win any of these tournaments can rest assured that their names will be remembered and revered for evermore in the pantheon of tennis greats.

If winning just one of these competitions remains the limit of many professionals' ambition, the absolute pinnacle of achievement is to win all four events in the same year. This is known as completing the Grand Slam, and is even more difficult than it sounds. Just staying fit and in top form is hard enough on the professional circuit, but to make things harder still, each of the Grand Slam events is contested on different surfaces - Wimbledon on grass, the US Open on cement, the French Open on clay, and the Australian Open on synthetic rubber. So anyone who achieves the Grand Slam can truly claim to be the best all-round tennis player of their generation.

The English tennis player Fred Perry was the first man to win all four events - albeit in different years. In 1938 the American Don Budge was the first man to achieve the Grand Slam proper, and only one man, the Australian Rod Laver, has done so since, in 1962 and 1969. Maureen Connolly was the first woman to achieve the feat in 1953, and this has only been repeated twice since - by Margaret Court in 1970 and by Steffi Graf in 1988.

Wimbledon

Wimbledon is the oldest and most prestigious of the Grand Slam events, and is played each year during the last week of June and the first week of July. The tennis may, in the minds of many impartial spectators, be peripheral to the champagne, the strawberries and the English social season, but the tournament remains the event that the players most want to win.

The first championships were held on the old Worple Road site of the All England Croquet and Lawn Tennis Club in 1877. This tournament was for men's singles only; women's singles and men's doubles were introduced in 1884, and it wasn't until 1913 that women's and mixed doubles were included. These are still the premier events, but nowadays the championships have expanded further to a total of 12 events, with various competitions for juniors and veterans thrown in to accommodate the ever-expanding world tennis circuit.

Twenty-two players entered the first Wimbledon, and the

winner was a man called Spencer Gore. It would be nice to record that he was a worthy winner and a devoted follower of the game, but, alas, it was not so. Thirteen years after making history, Mr Gore wrote: 'it is its want of variety that will prevent lawn tennis in its present form from taking rank among our great games'. The second winner, a P.F. Haddow, was little better. He only started playing tennis in the summer of 1878 while on holiday from Ceylon (as Sri Lanka was then known), where he worked as a tea planter. Having walked off with the tournament, he then walked away from the game. He never even watched another top-class tennis match until he was lured back to Wimbledon for the Silver Jubilee celebrations.

Luckily, things began to look up a little at this point, but the first true great did not appear until 1881 in the form of William Renshaw, who won the title seven times - still a record over the course of the decade. Even with the introduction of

the women's singles, first won by Maud Watson in 1884, the
tournament's fortunes flagged somewhat for a while in the late
nineteenth century, but the emergence of the Doherty brothers,
Laurie and Reggie, who dominated proceedings from 1897 to
1906, saw Wimbledon through to a pre-eminence from which
it has never looked back. Three Americans, James Dwight,
Richard Sears and A.L. Rives, became the first overseas
players in 1885, but it was not until 1900 that Marion Jones
became the first overseas women's entrant. Five years later
May Sutton became the first foreign winner, an event that has
become all too familiar to British eyes in the current post-war
period.

Until 1922, the winner of the previous year's tournament
automatically went through to contest the final of the next,
with all the other players being forced to play knock-out

challenge rounds to decide whom he or she should meet. In the same year that this archaic practice was abandoned, Wimbledon moved to the much larger site on Church Road, where it remains to this day, and in many ways the modern era of the tournament was born. The sex appeal and virtuosity of Suzanne Lenglen saw to it that every single one of her matches was played in front of full houses, and the public's enthusiasm for the women's game soon spilled over to the men's.

The men's game was dominated in the late 1920s by the French, in the shape of Borotra, Lacoste and Cochet, but apart from brief spells of British success with Kitty Godfree and Fred Perry in the mid-1930s, in the pre-war years thereafter both the men's and women's tournaments were largely the domain of the Americans. Post-war competition began again in 1946, even though part of the Centre Court was badly bomb-damaged. The first male post-war champion was a French ex-prisoner of war named Yvon Petra, but the late 1940s through to the late 1960s were generally characterised by the dominance of the Americans and the Australians.

In 1968 Wimbledon finally went open. The men's title deservedly went to Rod Laver, who had won the championship five years earlier whilst competing as an amateur, and since then Wimbledon has thrown up such great winners as Bjorn Borg, Martina Navratilova, Steffi Graf and Pete Sampras. And come the last week in June, every leading player in the world will be heading for south-west London dreaming of similar glory.

The US Open

If Wimbledon can lay claim to being the most prestigious event, then the US Open is certainly the toughest. For two weeks play begins at 10am and often goes through to midnight, so that matches begun in daylight end under floodlights; what's more, thanks to the demands of television and commercial sponsors, the men's semi-finals are always played the day before the final, giving precious little time for the players to rest in between. So, given that the tournament organisers make conditions so difficult, why do the players not boycott the event? The answer, of course, is part pride - the US is still a major championship - and part money - no Grand Slam event offers a bigger purse.

The first championship was held at Newport Casino, Rhode Island, in 1881, four years after the first Wimbledon, with Richard Sears emerging as the winner of the men's singles. A men's doubles event was also held at the same time, but it wasn't until 1887 that women's singles, doubles and mixed doubles became an established feature. Even then, these tournaments weren't held either at the same time or the same place; for some unfathomable reason, the organisers believed in segregating the sexes. Any events involving women were held at the Philadelphia Cricket Club, an anomaly that remained in force until 1921, when the women joined the men at their new (since 1915) venue of the West Side Club in Forest

The US Open is held at Flushing Meadow, New York

Hills, Long Island.

Even though overseas players were admitted to the tournament in 1884, Americans have always dominated the list of prize winners. In part this was by virtue of their talent - how can you argue against players of the talent of Bill Tilden, Helen Wills Moody, Hazel Wightman, Billie Jean King *et al*.? - but it was also in part due to the fact that until 1968, when the US went open, many foreign players did not bother to

make the journey across the Atlantic to participate.

Until 1974, the US championships were played on grass; however, unlike the Wimbledon courts, which were renowned for being in generally good condition, the courts at Forest Hills offered the players poor footholds, and the bounce of the ball was often extremely variable. Indeed, in the latter stages of the tournament there was so little grass left on the court that it was sprayed with green paint to present the illusion of an immaculate surface to the millions of television viewers around the world. In 1974, however, the organisers succumbed to the inevitable and dug up the court, replacing it with a clay one. This gave a much improved surface, but it did not go down too well with some of the home players, who thought that the court would be too similar to those found in Europe and would thus give the overseas players too great an advantage.

By the late 1970s it became obvious that the US Open had grown too big for the cramped surroundings of Forest Hills, and the organisers hunted around for a new home. A new site was hurriedly located and built at Flushing Meadow in New York City; the US Open moved there in 1978 and has remained there ever since. The new courts were made of acrylic cement, which produced a good bounce, and were roughly halfway in pace between clay and grass courts. This was clearly just what the doctor ordered as far as the home players were concerned, as they won most events in the early years of Flushing Meadow, but the 1980s saw a slight shift in balance towards the Europeans.

The US Open is far from genteel. The concrete stadia are brash and unattractive; the noise from the planes flying to and from La Guardia Airport is only matched by the vociferousness of the spectators - no hushed tones and reverent 'I says' for the Americans, thank you very much - and everywhere is permeated with the smell of hamburgers and hotdogs frying. But the tournament *is* exciting. It has always been innovative - it was the first to use a tie-break system - and the tennis is immensely competitive. The atmosphere is not to everyone's liking, but even so none of the top players would dream of missing it these days.

The French Open

There are few places more appealing in late May than Paris, and so it is perhaps understandable that of all the Grand Slam events, the French Open is the one most enjoyed by players and spectators alike. With its elegantly designed tennis courts at the Stade Roland Garros (named after the French World War I pilot who was killed in action in 1918) at Auteuil on the outskirts of Paris, and without the pressure of Wimbledon or the chaos of Flushing Meadow, the French Open has a relaxed atmosphere all of its own. Not too relaxed, mind, for the tournament is as hard-fought as any of the Grand Slam events.

Despite the pleasant surroundings, many players have consciously avoided the French Open. The tournament is played on clay, the slowest of all the surfaces; as such it places a premium on rally play and touch, and the big serve-and-volleyers who thrive elsewhere often come to grief if they are not capable of adjusting their style. So, rather than risk making a fool of themselves by being knocked out early and, worse still, slipping a few points down the computer rankings, some of the crash-bang merchants may invent convenient injuries.

But for all the absenteeism, the French Hall of Fame is a

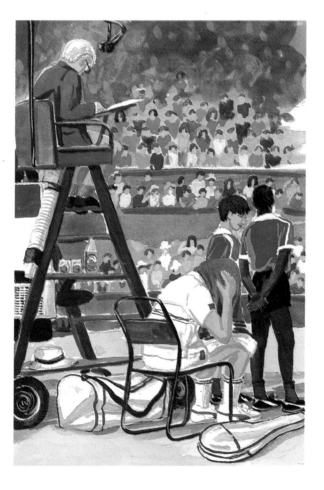

worthy one. If there are fewer American names on the men's trophy than one might expect, the roll-call still includes many of the all-time greats - Laver, Rosewall, Emerson, Cochet, Lacoste, von Cramm, Borg, Wilander, Santana, Drobny, Perry and Nastase, to name just some. But what the men's list lacks in Americans, the women's more than makes up for. American women have been far and away the most successful in Paris, with Chris Evert out on her own with seven victories. In recent years Steffi Graf has been homing in on that figure.

The first French championships were held in 1891, but they were restricted to French nationals and players registered to French clubs, and it wasn't until 1925 that the tournament was open to all comers and became truly international. At that time it was held at St Cloud in Paris, but it was only a couple of years before the venue was changed to the purpose-built Stade Roland Garros, where it has remained ever since. The French Open has never gained quite the cachet of Wimbledon or the US Open, but it deserves its place in the Grand Slam events. Quite apart from enjoying the delights of Paris in the spring, the winner can justifiably lay claim to being the best clay court specialist in the world.

The Australian Open

The biggest hurdle that the Australian Open has had to face is its location. Isolated many thousands of miles away from its three northern hemisphere Grand Slam partners, the Australian has always been looked upon rather as the Cinderella of the premier tournaments. Indeed, for a great many years a large number of players looked on Australia as simply too far away to be worth travelling to for competition, especially as the timing of the Australian summer (December - January) meant that many players were thinking more in terms of putting their feet up with their families over Christmas and taking a well-earned break from the rigours of the tour. But, without wishing to state the obvious, you can't win the Grand Slam without taking part, so anyone who has serious ambitions in that direction must travel south, and over the last 20 years or so the tournament has become a much more cosmopolitan event.

Australia has always had a long tradition of producing top tennis players, and it was primarily out of respect for this that the country's Open tournament became part of the Grand Slam. Even though the individual states had been holding their own tournaments since 1879, the first Australian national championships did not take place until 1905, when the country was recognised as a commonwealth. Unlike the other major tournaments, the Australian Open regularly changed venue: the Australian cities of Melbourne, Sydney, Brisbane and Perth were all blessed with fine grass courts and for many years the championships rotated between them. Indeed, on two occasions the tournament was held in New Zealand as, prior to 1925, it was known as the Australasian championships.

In 1970 the organisers decided just to alternate between Melbourne and Sydney, and two years later the glorious grass courts at Kooyong in Melbourne became the permanent home. By the 1980s, however, Kooyong was deemed to have become too small for a major tournament, and a new stadium with polyurethane and rubber playing surfaces was built at Flinders Park in Melbourne, where the tournament has been played since 1988.

The Australian Open has always struggled to find its identity. As a result it has often changed its format. In 1968 it dropped the mixed doubles from its programme, and in 1980 it went so far as to drop the women's events because it was felt that the women had been getting a raw deal in terms of media exposure and match scheduling. This only lasted for three years, however, as it was felt inappropriate for a Grand Slam event to promote segregated tennis. In 1987 mixed doubles was also restored to the tournament and the championships now run a full programme equal to Wimbledon, the US and the French.

There was a heavy preponderance of Australian winners in the pre-war years, a reflection of the low rate of foreign participation. But after the war, more and more international players made the journey to Australia, and since the championships went open in 1969 they have become truly cosmopolitan, and worthy of their place in the top four.

The Future

Tennis is no longer a game to the top professionals; it is big business. With sponsors queuing up to pay millions of dollars for the privilege of seeing their racket in Steffi Graf's hand and their logo on her skirt, Graf is almost a one-person multinational. Prize money of $350,000 for winning a top event may seem like a lot of money to the general public, but the prize money is only the tip of the iceberg. Win Wimbledon just once and a player need never 'work' again. But, of course, they do. They do it for the kudos and the acclaim, as well as the money.

But the game takes its toll. Steffi Graf had a tennis racket thrust into her hand at the age of three, and, ever since she was a teenager, has moved from hotel room to rented house and has few real friends. Sure, she's made a lot of money, but there is a high price to be paid for celebrity.

And Steffi got off remarkably lightly. Monica Seles was stabbed in the back by an obsessive fan, Jennifer Capriati was arrested on drugs and theft charges, and Tracy Austin has been almost crippled by a back condition brought on by playing too much tennis too young.

Tennis is a hard taskmaster, but there are hundreds of young hopefuls out there just waiting to step into the shoes of any professionals who fall off the treadmill. Increasingly, then, tennis will become the preserve of the young. It's not just the physical aspects that take their toll, it's the psychological ones too. Playing top-class tennis under the glare of the media month in, month out is a wearing experience, and it is expecting too much for players to carry on much beyond 30. Those that do survive will need to be mentally very tough.

Modern tennis, then, is a tough game, and has come a long way from the genteel recreational sport it started out as. Like all professional sports it demands practice and stamina, as well as talent, and expects a high level of committment from its exponents. But a glance at the local tennis courts on a fine summer's day will confirm that tennis is going from strength to strength and is definitely here to stay.